PENGUIN BOOKS

TWINKLE, TWINKLE, LITTLE STARS

Gervase Phinn is a teacher, freelance lecturer, author, poet, school inspector, educational consultant and visiting professor of education – but none of these is more important to him than his family.

For fourteen years he taught in a range of schools, then acted as General Adviser for Language Development in Rotherham before moving on to North Yorkshire, where he spent ten years as a school inspector – time that has provided so much source material for his books. He is a Fellow of the Royal Society of Arts and an Honorary Fellow of St John's College, York.

Gervase lives with his family near Doncaster.

Also by Gervase Phinn

THE DALES SERIES

The Other Side of the Dale
Over Hill and Dale
Head Over Heels in the Dales
Up and Down in the Dales
The Heart of the Dales

A Wayne in a Manger

POETRY
published by Puffin Books

It Takes One to Know One
The Day Our Teacher Went Batty
Family Phantoms
Don't Tell the Teacher

Twinkle, Twinkle, Little Stars

GERVASE PHINN

PENGUIN BOOKS

PENGUIN BOOKS

Published by the Penguin Group
Penguin Books Ltd, 80 Strand, London WC2R 0RL, England
Penguin Group (USA), Inc., 375 Hudson Street, New York, New York 10014, USA
Penguin Group (Canada), 90 Eglinton Avenue East, Suite 700, Toronto, Ontario, Canada M4P 2Y3
(a division of Pearson Penguin Canada Inc.)
Penguin Ireland, 25 St Stephen's Green, Dublin 2, Ireland (a division of Penguin Books Ltd)
Penguin Group (Australia), 250 Camberwell Road, Camberwell, Victoria 3124, Australia
(a division of Pearson Australia Group Pty Ltd)
Penguin Books India Pvt Ltd, 11 Community Centre, Panchsheel Park, New Delhi – 110 017, India
Penguin Group (NZ), 67 Apollo Drive, Rosedale, North Shore 0632, New Zealand
(a division of Pearson New Zealand Ltd)
Penguin Books (South Africa) (Pty) Ltd, 24 Sturdee Avenue, Rosebank,
Johannesburg 2196, South Africa

Penguin Books Ltd, Registered Offices: 80 Strand, London WC2R 0RL, England

www.penguin.com

First published by Michael Joseph 2008
Published in Penguin Books 2010

002

Book design by Janette Revill
Printed in Great Britain by Clays Ltd, St Ives plc

A CIP catalogue record for this book is available from the British Library

ISBN: 978–0–141–03643–4

www.greenpenguin.co.uk

Acknowledgements

The majority of these stories appeared originally in my five Dales books. However, for this special collection, I have embellished here, embroidered there, so these versions tend to be a variation on the originals.

The poems first appeared in the four collections published by Puffin Books, and are reproduced with their kind permission; there have been a few changes to the poems.

From *It Takes One to Know One*: 'The Way I Am', 'Farmboy' (originally 'Farmgirl'), 'Class Discussion' and 'Bible Class'.

From *The Day Our Teacher Went Batty*: 'Angel in the Cloakroom', 'Dreaming' and 'Spelling'.

From *Don't Tell the Teacher*: 'Home', 'Question' and 'Using Your Imagination'.

CONTENTS

GERVASE

I was not a particularly clever or confident child, never the bright little button who sat on the top table with all the clever children, with his hand always in the air to answer the teacher's questions, the talented artist, sharp at number work, the good speller, the one who won all the cups, captained the school team, took the lead part in the school play. I was a member of the unremarkable majority – the average pupil, the big hump in the academic bell, the 'nothing special' sort of child, ordinary, biddable, quiet.

Last year I visited my former infant school headmistress, the redoubtable Miss Wilkinson. She was a 101 years old but still had the shining eyes of the great teacher.

'You have done very well, Gervase,' she said, shaking my hand. 'All those books you have written. Doctor this and professor that – you have more degrees than a thermometer.' Then she added with a twinkle in those shining eyes, 'And you were never one of the brightest in the class, were you?'

'No, I wasn't,' I replied. 'I suppose I was a pretty average child but if I've achieved anything in life it is because of my parents and teachers like you who believed in me and encouraged me.'

'And you do recall,' she asked, 'when you wet yourself?'

'Of course,' I replied. The occasion remains ingrained in my memory.

At the infant nativity play, I was one of the extras. The curtains opened and there I stood, on the otherwise empty stage, next to the cardboard stable, six years old and stiff as a lamp-post. I was the palm tree. I was encased in brown crêpe paper with two big bunches of papier mâché coconuts dangling from my neck, a clump of bright green cardboard leaves in each hand and more arranged like a crown on my head. My mother had knitted me a pale green woollen balaclava helmet through which my little face peeped. I was so excited and stared out at all the faces in the audience.

Then someone in the front row laughed and that started off others laughing, too. They were laughing at *me*! It was the first occasion anyone had laughed at me and I felt so alone and upset and had wriggled nervously. I looked for my parents and, seeing them in the second row, I focused on them. They, of course, were not laughing. I began to cry and then, frozen under the bright lights and frightened, I wet myself. It seeped through the brown crêpe paper, leaving a large dark stain in the front. The audience laughed louder. I was devastated.

On the way home, my face wet with tears, my father held my small hand between his great fat fingers and he told me that I was the best palm tree he had ever seen. My mother told me that I was the star of the show. I knew full well at the time that they were not telling me the truth, but it was so good to be told. I felt so secure and so loved.

'And do you remember, Miss Wilkinson,' I asked her now, 'what you said to me when I came off the stage? Instead of being cross, and telling me I should have gone to the toilet before the show, as some teachers might well have done, you put your arm round me and said, "Don't worry, love, it's not the end of the world. Why, when I was your age, I used to wet my knickers, too."' There was a short silence. Then a small smile came to my former teacher's lips. 'It's funny how things come full circle.'

In this collection of stories, anecdotes and poems, the shining stars are the children, all of whom I met over my years as a schools inspector in the great county of Yorkshire. They will, I hope, delight you as they did me, with their blunt observations on life, their disarming honesty and their irrepressible humour. For me, whatever their background and abilities, they will forever be my bright little stars.

☆ I ☆

THE WAY I AM

I'm just an ordinary sort of boy,
Not the centre of attention,
The best of the bunch,
Apple of the teacher's eye,
The one everyone remembers.
It's just the way I am.

I'm just an ordinary sort of boy,
Not the high flyer,
Captain of the team,
Star of the school play,
Top of the class.
It's just the way I am.

I'm just an ordinary sort of boy,
But I'm not invisible.
I do exist!
I'm as different as anyone else,
There's nobody like me.
And to my family, I'm pretty special.
So please, sir, please, miss – notice ME sometimes.
I am what I am.

☆ 2 ☆

TRACEY
ASKS QUESTIONS

I was accompanying the new Chairman of the Education Committee around a village primary school. He was certainly viewed with much interest when he entered the small classroom and, with his red cheeks, great walrus moustache and hair shooting up from his square head, it was not surprising. He was introduced to the very nervous teacher who was taking the class, and then sat down solidly, legs apart, on a tiny red melamine chair designed for very small children.

After a while he was approached by Tracey, a little girl who stared and stared at his round, red face and drooping moustache. Then the following conversation took place.

'What is it?' asked the little girl.

'What's what?' retorted the visitor.

'That on your face.'

'It's a moustache.'

'What does it do?'

'It doesn't do anything.'

'Oh.'

'It just sits there on my lip.'

'Does it go up your nose?'

'No.'
'Could I stroke it?'
'No.'
'Is it alive?'
'No, it's not alive.'
'Can I have one?'
'No.'
'Why?'
'Well, little girls don't have moustaches.'
'Why?'
'Because they don't.'
'Can I have one when I grow up?'
'No.'
'Why not?'
'Because ladies don't have moustaches either.'
The little girl thought for a moment, tilted her head on one side before answering. 'Well, my grannie's got one!'

☆ 3 ☆

OLIVER
AND THE SCHOOL SUSPECTOR

The children sat straight-backed and silent at their desks, looking nervously at me. Their teacher – a tall, thin woman with a pale melancholic face, and dressed in a prim white blouse buttoned up to the neck – scanned her class with an expression that would freeze soup in cans.

'Mr Phinn is a school inspector,' she told the children. 'He will be testing your reading this afternoon.' She turned in my direction and in a sharp voice announced, 'They are very good at reading, Mr Phinn.'

'I am sure they are,' I replied.

'And you will find that they are competent, too, at arithmetic.' She turned to the class and fixed them with a gimlet eye. 'Are you not, children?'

'Yes, miss,' they chorused unenthusiastically.

'And I bet you have a lot of fun in school,' I said. I didn't mean to sound sarcastic but, judging from the teacher's expression, it must have appeared like that.

'Mr Phinn,' she said with a slight smile, 'we do have a lot of fun in this school.' She stared at her class. 'Don't we, children?' The children stared impassively. 'We really do have so much fun, don't we?' she repeated a little louder.

There were a few nods. I caught sight of a small studious-looking little boy at the back with large glasses and a mop of unruly red hair. He shook his head. The teacher had spotted him, too.

'Yes, we do, Oliver! We're always having fun.' She fixed him with a rattle-snake look and gave a little laugh. It was not a pleasant little laugh. 'Too much to say for himself, that young man, Mr Phinn,' the teacher confided in me in an undertone. 'We do have a lot of fun.'

As I passed Oliver on my way out, I heard him mutter, 'I must have been away that day.' I suppressed a smile.

'Oliver,' continued the teacher quickly, her face now rather more leering than smiling and her voice with quite a sharpness of tone to it, 'would you go and ask the school secretary to ring the bell for dinnertime, please, there's a good boy.' The last phrase was said with some emphasis. 'And shall we all now say "Goodbye" to Mr Phinn, children?'

'Goodbye, Mr Phinn,' the class intoned.

'Goodbye,' I said.

Oliver and I walked down the corridor together. 'Can I ask you something, Mr Phinn?' he said.

'Of course.'

'How do you become one of these suspectors, then?'

'Inspectors, Oliver.'

'How do you become one?'

'Well, you have to work hard at school, read a lot of books and when you go up to the big school you have to pass your exams and that takes a long, long time.'

'How old do you have to be?' he asked.

'You have to be twenty-one to be a teacher, even older to be a school inspector, so you have a long way to go.'

'And then you can sit at the back of classrooms and watch people?'

'That's right.'

'And hear children read?'

'That's right.'

'And look at their writing?'

'And look at their writing,' I repeated.

The little boy looked up and then scratched at the shock of red hair. 'And you get paid for it?'

'And you get paid for it,' I told him. He still looked very thoughtful, so I said: 'Would you like to ask me anything else?'

'No, not really, but . . .' He paused.

'Go on, Oliver. Have you got something to tell me?'

'Well, Mr Phinn, I was just thinking, that when I'm twenty-one, you'll probably be dead!'

☆ 4 ☆

CHLOË
AND THE CHICKS

In the Infant classroom, I discovered Miss Reece, a young woman with sandy-coloured hair tied back in a pony tail and wearing a bright yellow mohair jumper and pale cream slacks. She sat with the children clustered around her and was reading them a story from a large coloured picture book which was displayed on an easel beside her. One small girl sat on her knee. I crept to the back of the classroom, perched on a small melamine chair and listened.

'I can see the little lamb bleating in the meadow,' read the teacher slowly and dramatically. She pointed at the picture. 'Can you see the little lamb, children? Isn't he lovely and woolly?' The children nodded vigorously. Miss Reece continued, 'I can see the little calf mooing for his mother.'

'He's black and white, miss,' volunteered the child sitting on the teacher's knee.

'He is, isn't he, Chloë.' The teacher read on. 'I can see the little foal frisking in the field. "Frisking" is an unusual word, isn't it, children?'

'It means kicking up its legs, Miss Reece,' called out a child sitting cross-legged in front of her.

'Well done, Martin. It does mean that.'

'He's sweet, isn't he, miss?' said the little girl sitting on the teacher's knee.

'He is very sweet, Chloë,' agreed the teacher, 'but just listen, dear, there's a good girl, otherwise we will never get to the end.' She turned the page. 'I can see the little piglet grunting in the grass.'

A small boy, with red hair and a runny nose, who was sitting directly in front of me, began snorting and grunting like a pig.

'We don't need the animal noises, John-Paul, thank you very much,' said the teacher with a slight edge to her voice. 'Just look at the pictures and listen to the words.' She turned the page. 'I can see the little chicks chirping in the farmyard.' The small child sitting on the teacher's knee leaned forward and looked intently at the picture of the bright yellow chicks. 'They look as if they have just hatched out of their eggs, don't they, children?' said the teacher. 'All soft and fluffy and golden.'

Chloë looked at the picture and then at the teacher and then back at the picture. After a moment she began stroking the teacher's bright yellow mohair jumper.

'Do you know, miss,' she said in that loud, confident voice only possessed by young children, 'you look as if you've just been laid.'

Miss Reece turned crimson and I nearly fell off the chair, laughing.

☆ 5 ☆

JOHN
HAS A MIDNIGHT SURPRISE

John was a serious little boy of about seven or eight, with tangled straw-coloured hair. I had been reading the story of Peter Rabbit in Mr McGregor's garden to his class, and young John had spoken up, saying rabbits were a nuisance and should be shot.

In the break that followed, his teacher, Mrs Brown, told me that John lived on a farm way out at the other side of the dale. It was a hard but happy life he led. He was expected, like most children from farming families, to help around the farm before he went to school and when he got home. He was a shrewd, good-natured, blunt-speaking little boy with a host of stories to tell about farm life. The following story, however, had been told to Mrs Brown by John's father.

When he was little, Mrs Brown told me, John was woken by his father in the middle of the night. The child was wrapped up warmly and carried across the yard to the byre. The vet had suggested to John's father that it was about time the boy saw the miracle of nature: the birth of a calf.

In the cattle shed, one solitary bulb threw a subdued light and cast dancing shadows on the wooden walls, and the place smelt of silage and animal warmth. His father placed the child on a bale of hay.

'Now, young man,' the vet said, 'when I was your age and saw what you will see tonight, it changed my life and made

me want to become a vet. I want you to be very quiet and soon you will see something wonderful.'

The child peered into the half-light as the great black Angus cow strained to deliver her calf. In due course, the small, wet, furry bundle arrived and the vet, glowing with perspiration but with a triumphant look on his face, gently wiped the calf's mouth and then held up the new-born creature under the flickering light for the little boy to see. The calf glistened in the brightness. John stared wide-eyed.

'What do you think of that?' the vet asked him. 'Isn't that a wonderful sight?'

The boy thought for a moment before replying. 'So how did it swallow the dog in the first place?'

☆ 6 ☆

FARMBOY

When he's collected the eggs
And milked the cows,
Groomed the mare
And fed the sows,
Filled the troughs
And stacked the logs,
Cooped the hens
And penned the dogs . . .
He then begins his homework.

☆ 7 ☆

TREVOR
MEETS ROYALTY

The royal visitor, accompanied by the Mayor, the High Sheriff, the Lord Lieutenant and other assorted dignitaries, walked along the line of children waving flags and holding out bunches of flowers. She looked every inch the princess, beautifully dressed, slim and elegant and with a stunning smile. It was clear she had a rapport with the children for she would stop and talk to them, bending low so she was at eye level, shaking little hands and receiving bunch after bunch of flowers which she passed back to her lady-in-waiting.

At the very end of the line stood a small boy. He had a mop of dusty brown hair and a little green candle was emerging from his crusty nostril. Wide-eyed, the child held out two wilting blooms.

The royal visitor smiled warmly and took the flowers from him.

'Thank you,' she said, leaning close to him and patting him on the head. 'And what's your name?'

'Trevor,' the child replied.

'And have you had the day off school, Trevor,' she asked, 'especially to come and see me?'

'No,' he replied, scratching his scalp, 'I've been sent home because I've got nits.'

☆ 8 ☆

MAXINE
AND THE BIG STICK

The school was a relatively modern building in honey-coloured brick with an orange pantile roof and large picture windows. It was surrounded by fields and rocky outcrops and backed by a friendly belt of larch and spruce trees which climbed towards the high moors. Everything about it looked clean and well tended. I, the school inspector, arrived just before morning playtime and heard the squealing and laughing of small children as they ran and played in the schoolyard.

I was just about to enter the main door when a very distressed-looking little girl of about five or six, her face wet with weeping and her cheeks smeared where little hands had tried to wipe away the tears, tugged at my jacket.

'They've all got big sticks!' she wailed piteously.

'Who's got big sticks?' I asked, surprised.

'All on 'em. They've all got big sticks!'

'Well, they shouldn't have big sticks,' I replied.

'I want a big stick!' she cried, sniffing and sobbing, her little body shaking in anguish.

'No, you can't have a big stick. It's very dangerous.'

'I want a big stick!' she cried. 'I want a big stick!'

'You could hurt somebody with a big stick,' I said.

'But they've all got big sticks!' she howled again. 'They've all got 'em.'

At this point the headteacher appeared from the direction of the playground.

'Whatever is it, Maxine?' she asked, gently pulling the little body towards her like a hen might comfort a chick.

The small child clutching her began to moan and groan again pitifully. 'I want a big stick, Miss Bentley,' she moaned. 'They've all got big sticks.'

'Of course you can have one,' the headteacher replied, wiping away the little girl's tears. 'You weren't there when I gave everybody one. You don't think I'd leave you out, Maxine, do you? You come with me and I'll get you one, a nice big one. How about that? I won't be a moment, Mr Phinn.'

'A big stick?' I murmured. 'You're giving this little girl a big stick?'

The headteacher gave a great grin before replying, 'She means a biscuit.'

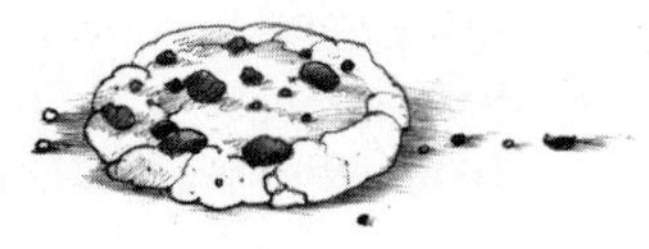

☆ 9 ☆

ELIZABETH
AT THE OPTICIAN'S

My visit to the infant school was to test the children's reading. I met Elizabeth in that part of the classroom called the Home Corner, where children can dress up, get into role, practise talking, reading, writing and acting out parts. The teacher confided in me later that she had chuckled when a rather pompous inspector had once referred to this area as the Social Interaction Centre. The Home Corner in this classroom was set out like an optician's shop. There were posters and signs, price lists and eye charts, a small desk with plastic till, appointment book and a large red telephone. Elizabeth was dressed in one of her daddy's white shirts. She had a piece of string around her neck attached to a pair of empty frames and was busy arranging some spectacles on a small stand. She was the first child due to be tested for reading so I approached.

'Hello,' I greeted her amiably.

'Oh hello,' she replied cheerily and popped the frames on the end of her nose. 'Is it a pair of glasses you want?'

I hadn't the heart to say, 'No, I'm here to give you the Cathcart-Smitt Reading Test,' so I replied, 'Yes, that's right.'

'What sort have you in mind?'

'I think I'd like a pair which makes me look considerably younger.'

'Well, we'll see what we can do.' Then she added, 'I shall have to test your eyes, you know.'

'I thought you might,' I replied.

'Can you read?'

Here was the school inspector come to test the child's reading and he was being tested himself. I nodded and was presented with a list of letters which I read as she pointed to each in turn.

'You have very good eyes,' she said as she rummaged in a box of frames. 'And you want some to make you look young?' She finally decided on a pair as pink as elastoplast, pointed at the ends, with diamanté studs. I tried them on and looked in the mirror. Elizabeth watched fascinated for a moment and then began giggling. She slapped her hand over her mouth to stop herself but her little body shook with mirth.

'Are you laughing at me?' I asked sadly, peering through the ridiculous pair of glasses.

She nodded slowly and stopped giggling.

'And are you the manageress of this optician's shop?'

She nodded again, her face taking on a slightly quizzical expression. She really did not know what to make of me.

'I don't think it's very nice of you to laugh at your customers.' I pulled a strained face. 'I'm very upset.'

She stared for a moment before approaching me and then, patting me lightly on the arm, whispered gently, 'It's only pretend, you know.'

☆ 10 ☆

HOME

In the Home Corner,
In an infant school classroom,
A boy and girl,
Rising five,
Were arguing.
Stabbing the air with small fingers,
Jutting out their chins,
And stamping little feet.
'Oh, do shut up!'
'No, you shut up!'
'I'm sick of you!'
'And I'm sick of you!'
'Oh, just be quiet!'
'No, you be quiet!'
'Oh, do shut up!'
'No, you shut up!'
'What's all this?' the teacher cried.
'We're playing mums and dads,'
The infants both replied.

☆ **II** ☆

ANDREW
THE SHEEP EXPERT

It was at the end of the day when I joined a sturdy-looking little boy with a healthy complexion who was standing at the classroom window, hands deep in his pockets, surveying the vast panorama which stretched out before him. He was about six or seven years old.

'Just waiting for mi mam to come,' he told me. 'She's offen a bit late. She 'as a lot to do on t'farm.'

'Well, I'm sure she'll not be long,' I said.

'Aye, well, I'm not goin' anyweer.'

'Beautiful view,' I said.

'It's not bad, int it?' He dug his hands deeper into his pockets. 'Autumn's comin' on,' observed the child like a little old man. 'Not be long afoor t'bracken turns gowld and t'leaves start to fall. Looks like it's gunna be a bad winter an' all. We 'ad a lot of snow last year. Mi dad can't be doin' wi' snow.'

'I'm not over keen,' I said. 'And what's your name?'

'Andrew.'

'Well, it's certainly a beautiful view, Andrew,' I said. 'You're a lucky boy to live up here.'

'Aye, as I said, it's all reight. Better in t'summer than winter though, when tha can get out and about. Starts about this time o' year, does winter, when it gets cowld and wet and windy.'

'And what do you like best at school?' I asked.

'I likes to read and I likes number work. I'm good at sums.'

'Are you?' I thought I'd test him on his arithmetic. 'How many sheep can you see in that field?' I asked him.

'Eh?'

'Can you tell me how many sheep you can see in the field?'

'Aye, I can.'

'Well, how many can you see?'

'I can see all on 'em,' he replied.

I chuckled. 'No, I meant how many altogether. Could you count them for me?'

'Aye, I suppose I could. I'm good at countin'.'

'Perhaps you'd like to show me,' I persisted.

'Well, there's five Swaledales and six Texels, three hybrids and four hoggits.' He paused for a moment. 'That makes eighteen in total, dunt it? And don't ask me to count t'rabbits because they waint stay still long enough for me to tot 'em up.' A large and rusty old Land Rover pulled up outside the school gate. 'Hey up, mi mam's 'ere.' With a wave he scurried off. 'Ta-ra!'

BAA
166

☆ 12 ☆

BILLY
MAKING BABIES

'And what is your name, young man?' I asked the small, rosy-cheeked boy who stood by the classroom window.

'Mi mam calls me William an' mi dad calls me Billy,' he told me.

'And what shall I call you?' I asked.

'Tha can suit thissen, mester, I'll answer to owther,' he replied.

'Well, Billy, you certainly live in one of the most beautiful parts of Yorkshire,' I told him.

'Do I?'

'Of course.' I gestured out of the classroom window. 'Just take a look at that spectacular view.'

'What's so special abaat t'view then?' he asked bluntly.

I described for him the magnificent panorama which lay before us. 'Just look for a moment, Billy,' I said, 'really look. See the distant purple fells shrouded in a fleecy mist, the pine-scented woodland stretching around in a dark green belt, the undulating green of the dale flecked with cold winter sunshine and dotted with lazy-looking sheep.' The little boy stared up at me as if I were from another planet and then back at the view. 'Pause a moment, Billy,' I continued, 'and see the little rusty-red beck which trickles between the silvered limestone walls creviced with tiny pink gillyflowers. Don't you think it's a wonderful sight?'

''Appen,' he said.

I smiled. Yorkshire people are plain speaking and often not ones to use an excess of words.

'I wish I lived here,' I said.

'I know 'ow to mek babies,' he suddenly announced.

'Pardon?'

'Babies. I know 'ow to mek 'em. I learnt yesterday.'

'Really.'

'Aye. I know 'ow to do it now.'

'Good,' I said simply. I really did not wish to pursue this line of conversation.

I have met many a young person on my travels as a school inspector and been delighted by their humour, intrigued by their responses to my questions and amused by their sharp observations on life. But on a few rare occasions, like this one, I have been completely lost for words. A colleague had warned me early on in my career about such potentially hazardous situations. He had told me, that when faced with an inquisitive child who asks a tricky question or raises an embarrassing topic, to smile widely, nod sagely and be as evasive as possible. So that is what I did with little Billy. But the child persisted.

'So,' he said, 'do you know how to mek babies, mester?'

'Yes, I do,' I told him.

'Well, how do you mek babies, then?' he asked, looking up at me.

'You go first,' I said.

'Well,' said the boy, sucking in his bottom lip, 'I knock off the "y" and put "ies". That's 'ow I mek babies.'

☆ 13 ☆

JANICE

AND THE LITTLE LAMBS

Janice was a large healthy-looking girl sporting straw-coloured hair gathered up in enormous bushy bunches. She deposited her reading book and folder of written work in front of me, plopped onto the chair and stared up with a wearisome expression on her round face. It was clear that this pupil was not overly enthusiastic about showing me her work but she was by no means daunted by the presence of the stranger in the dark suit.

I smiled. 'And what is your name?'

'Janice.'

'Well, Janice, I'm Mr Phinn and I am here to see how well you are getting on in school.' She nodded. 'And how do you think you are getting on?'

'All reight,' she replied somewhat sullenly.

'Working hard?'

'Yeah.'

'And keeping up with the work?'

'Yeah.'

'And what do you enjoy best about school?'

'Goin' 'ome,' she told me bluntly.

'Well, would you like to read to me?'

'I'm not dead keen, but I will if I 'ave to.' She picked up the reading book in front of her. I saw it was called *An Anthology of Animal Verse.*

'Ah, a poetry book. Do you like poetry then, Janice?'

'Not really,' replied the girl, then added: 'It's just that poems are shorter than stories and easier to read.'

She chose to read a poem called *Nature's Treasure.* It was delivered slowly and loudly, the reader stabbing the words with a large finger like someone tapping out an urgent Morse code message.

Oh, what lovely little lambs
Prancing in the spring.
Hear their happy bleating,
Oh, what joy they bring!

I groaned inwardly and had to sit through six more verses, all as trite as the first.

'Is that it, then?' asked Janice, snapping the book shut and looking up at me. She was clearly keen to get away. I suggested that she might like to tell me a little about what she had just read.

She considered the prospect for a moment before replying. 'I 'ave enough trouble wi' readin' it, ne'er mind havin' to tell you abaat it as well.'

'Do you like reading then, Janice?' I asked cheerfully.

'No.'

I gave it up as a bad job. 'Well, shall we look at your written work?'

'Can if tha wants.'

Janice's written work consisted largely of spelling exercises, short pedestrian passages of prose, a few poor-quality rhyming poems and numerous accounts, rather more lively and descriptive, of calving, lambing, sheep-shearing and other farming matters.

'You keep cows on your farm then, do you, Janice?'

'Yeah.'

'And pigs?'

'Yeah.'

'And what about sheep?'

'What about 'em?'

'Do you have any?'

'Yeah.'

This was hard work but I persevered. 'And do you help with the lambing?' I asked.

'Yeah.'

'It must be wonderful each year to see those little woolly creatures, like the ones in the poem, all wet and steaming in the morning air, with their soft fleeces, black eyes like shiny beads and their tails flicking and twitching.'

'It's all reight,' she said, stifling a yawn.

'And what do you like best about lambing?'

She considered me again with the doleful eyes before telling me without batting an eyelid, 'Best part's when me and mi brother slide on t'afterbirth in t'yard.'

☆ 14 ☆

FRED

CAFÉ OWNER

In the Home Corner, set out as Fred's Café, I met a stocky six-year-old boy wearing a large blue apron over his school clothes. He was playing the part of Fred, the

café proprietor. All around him were notices and signs: NO DOGS ALLOWED, SPECIAL OF THE WEEK, COD 'N' CHIPS, NO SMOKING!, WAITER SERVICE. I seated myself at the small table and looked at a blank piece of paper at the top of which was written in bold lettering: MENU.

The little boy sidled up and stared at me intently. I looked up.

'What's it to be?' he asked.

'Oh,' I said, taking on the role of a customer, 'I think I'll just have something to drink.'

'Anything to eat?'

'No, I don't think so.'

'So you just want a drink?'

'Yes, please.'

'What about some fish an' chips?'

'No, I'm really not that hungry.'

'Just a drink?'

'That's right.'

The boy disappeared and returned a moment later with a small, empty plastic beaker which he placed before me. Then he watched intently as I drank the imaginary liquid, licked my lips and exclaimed, 'That was the nicest cup of tea I have had in a long while.'

'It was an 'arf o' bitter,' he told me bluntly and walked off.

☆ 15 ☆

SOPHIA
A NEW GIRL

I was surrounded by a group of ten-year-old children in the Junior School classroom. They sat quietly at their desks as I told them the story of David and Goliath, of how the young shepherd boy with only a sling and a pebble defeated the champion of the Philistines. All the children, with the exception of just one, listened in rapt attention, their eyes widening at the part where Goliath, in his bronze armour and with his great spear, roared at David: 'I will give your body to the birds and animals to eat!' Their facial expressions changed with the story and there was an audible sigh at the end when the Israelites cheered their champion who had killed the giant and saved his people.

The exception was a small, serious-faced girl whose big eyes bulged unblinkingly. She sat right under my nose, her hands resting gently on the desk, her face expressionless. I was intrigued. When I finished the story, I asked her, 'And what is your name?'

'Sophia,' she replied quietly, without a trace of a smile.

'Did you like the story?' She nodded. 'Did Goliath frighten you a little bit at the beginning?' She nodded. 'And did you feel happy at the end?' She nodded.

Then I caught sight of the teacher at the back of the room, smiling widely. Her expression said: 'Let the inspector get out of this one.'

It was obvious to me that this girl did not find it easy to communicate. English was, no doubt, her second or third language. I had been told by the headteacher that several of the children in the school had only recently arrived from Eastern Europe and had a very limited command of English, but that they were keen, well behaved and were learning fast. I was also told that some of the children in this class had special educational needs and had problems with reading and writing.

I tried again. 'Did you think Goliath would win?' She nodded. 'Have you heard any other Bible stories?' She nodded. 'Can you think of a word to describe Goliath?' She nodded. I mouthed the words slowly and deliberately. 'WHAT – WORD – COMES – INTO – YOUR – HEAD – WHEN – YOU – THINK – OF – GOLIATH?' She stared up at me without blinking. I tried again. 'AT – THE – BEGINNING – WHAT – WORD,' I tapped my forehead, 'WHAT – WORD – COMES – INTO – YOUR – HEAD?' She continued to stare. My voice rose an octave. 'WHAT – WORD – COMES – INTO – YOUR – HEAD – WHEN – YOU – THINK – OF – THE – GIANT – AT – THE – BEGINNING – OF – THE – STORY?'

After a thoughtful pause, the girl said in a clear and confident voice and with a slight smile on her face: 'Well, I should say aggressive.'

☆ 16 ☆

CLASS DISCUSSION

'In the class discussion, dear, you hardly said a word.
We all aired our opinions but from you we rarely heard.
You sat and stared in silence, surrounded by the chatter,
Now tell me, dear, and please be plain,
Is there anything the matter?'

The child looked up and then she spoke,
Her voice was clear and low:
'There are many people in this world
Who are rather quiet, you know!'

☆ 17 ☆

NAOMI
AND THE WOBBLING GRANNY

'Would you like me to read to you?' asked a small girl, with wide, cornflower-blue eyes and a mass of blonde hair which was gathered in two large candyfloss bunches.

'Yes,' I replied, 'I would like that very much.'

'I'm a very good reader, you know,' she confided in me, while she searched in her bag for her book.

'Are you?'

'I read with expression.'

'Do you?'

'And I can do different voices.'

'Really? I expect you use dramatic pauses as well,' I said mischievously.

She looked up for a moment and then added seriously, 'I don't know what they are, but I probably can.'

She was indeed a very accomplished little reader and sailed through her book confidently and fluently. 'I *am* good, aren't I?' she announced when she had completed three pages.

'Very good,' I said.

'I'm good at writing as well.'

'I imagined you would be.'

'Would you like to see my writing?'

'I'd love to.'

'Poetry or prose?'

'Poetry, please.'

'I keep my poems in a portfolio.'

'I guessed you would,' I said, smiling.

Her writing was neat, imaginative and accurate. 'I *am* good at writing, aren't I?'

'Very good,' I agreed.

'I'm good at talking as well.'

'I can tell that. I think your mummy's got a little chatterbox at home.'

'Oh, no!' exclaimed the child. 'My granny has asthma and I'm not allowed to keep pets.'

'I see,' I said, chuckling. I couldn't imagine what sort of animal she thought a 'little chatterbox' was.

'My granny calls me her "bright little button".'

'That's a lovely name,' I told her. 'They're very special, are grannies, and we must really look after them.'

'My granny wobbles, you know,' the little chatterbox continued.

'Does she?'

'She has a special disease which makes her wobble and forget things.'

'I'm sorry to hear that.'

'Yes,' said the little girl, nodding sagely. 'It's called "Old Timers' Disease".'

I chuckled.

'Why are you laughing?' she said, her little brow furrowing. 'It's not funny, you know, having "Old Timers' Disease".'

'Indeed, it's not,' I told the child and thinking to myself that when I'm feeble, old and grey, I would like my children to say that their father has got 'Old Timers' Disease'. It sounds much more friendly and humane than Alzheimer's Disease.

☆ 18 ☆

RICHARD
AND THE COOKERY CLASS

The school kitchen was a hive of activity. Two boys, smart in white aprons, were helping a large woman with floury hands take their culinary efforts out of the oven. One boy had such a dusting of flour on his face that he looked like Marley's ghost.

'Do you like tarts?' he asked as I approached.

'Pardon?'

'Tarts. Do you like tarts?'

'Jam tarts,' added the teacher with the floury hands, winking at me.

'Oh, I'm very partial to tarts.'

'Do you want one of mine?'

'I think our visitor might enjoy one of your tarts at afternoon break, Richard, with his cup of tea.' There was a look on the teacher's face which recommended me not to eat one of the tarts on offer.

'But I want to know what he thinks,' the boy told her.

'You have to wait until they are cool, Richard.'

'Tarts are better when they're hot, miss,' persisted the boy. He then looked at me with a shining, innocent face.

'Don't *you* think hot tarts are much better than cold ones?'

'I do,' I agreed, 'and I will have one of your tarts now.' The teacher's face took on an expression which told me that I had been warned.

The boy selected the biggest on the baking tray – a large, crusty-looking, misshapen lump of pastry. In the centre was a blob of dark red which I supposed was jam. It looked the most unappetizing piece of pastry I had ever seen, but I could not go back now. The boy watched keenly as I took a massive bite.

'What do you think?' asked the boy eagerly.

It was extremely difficult to speak as the dried-up confection coated the inside of my mouth. I coughed and sprayed the air with bits of pastry and dried jam. 'I have never tasted a tart like this in my life,' I assured him honestly, between splutters.

A great smile spread across the boy's face. 'Really?'

'Really.'

'Would you like another?'

'No, thank you,' I replied quickly. 'Delicious though it was, one is quite enough.'

At the end of the afternoon, as I was heading for the door, the little chef appeared with a brown paper bag in his hand.

'I've put another of my tarts in here for you,' he said, 'to have with your tea tonight.'

'That's very kind,' I said. 'Thank you very much.'

'Funny thing is baking, isn't it?' the boy pondered, holding out his hands in front of him the better to examine them. 'You know, my hands were dead mucky before I started making my tarts and just look how clean they are now.'

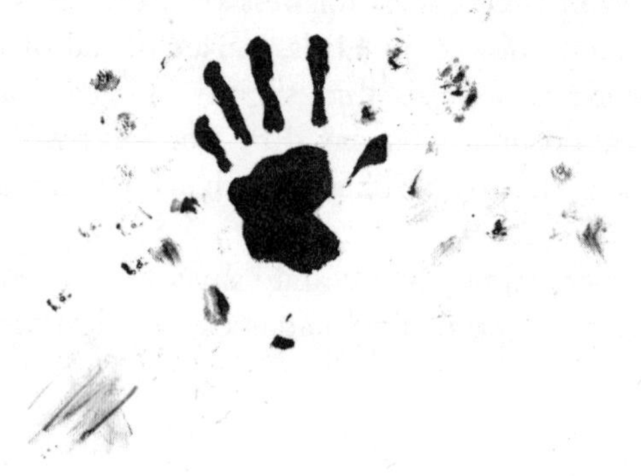

☆ 19 ☆

CRESSIDA
FACES THE MUSIC

Miss Bronson, headmistress of the Lady Cavendish High School for Girls, walked ahead of me down the corridor. She was a thin, slightly stooped woman with a pale indrawn face, narrow dark eyes and thick iron-grey hair cut in a bob. A voluminous black gown was draped around her shoulders.

'Do come along, Mr Phinn,' she said in a very upper-class accent. 'I would like you to see how I deal with a recalcitrant student.'

I was intrigued.

We soon arrived at the girls' cloakroom. Standing outside, looking extremely ill at ease, was a tall fair-haired girl in a smart dark green pinafore dress and pristine white blouse. She certainly did not look at all like a recalcitrant student.

'Now, Cressida,' said the headmistress, pulling an appropriately shocked face, 'so you are the culprit?'

'Yes, Miss Bronson,' replied the girl quietly.

'This gentleman with me,' she told her, 'is Mr Phinn. He is a school inspector.'

The girl stared at me with a terrified expression.

'Don't worry, he is not here to take you away,' the

headmistress told her, with a small smile playing on her lips. 'He is here to see how I deal with poorly behaved students.'

'Miss Bronson –' began the girl.

The headmistress held up a hand as if stopping traffic. 'Silence!'

At this moment, the caretaker – a sullen-looking individual in a shapeless grey overall and sporting bright yellow rubber gloves – appeared. He carried a large sponge.

'Thank you for joining us, Mr Merryman,' said the headmistress. 'This will not take long.' She turned to the student. 'Now, Cressida, perhaps you would like to acquaint Mr Phinn with what you have been doing?'

'Kissing the mirror,' mumbled the girl.

'Speak up, Cressida,' said the headmistress.

'I've been kissing the mirror in the cloakroom,' she told me, shamefaced.

'She's been kissing the mirror,' repeated the headmistress. 'Do you know, Mr Phinn, at the end of the day, this young lady has been putting on her make-up in the cloakroom and leaving behind large red marks where she has kissed the mirror. I can't for the life of me understand why anyone would want to kiss a mirror.'

'I was practising, miss,' the girl informed her.

'Practising?' repeated the headmistress, looking like a startled cat. 'Practising for what?'

The girl remained silent.

'Practising for what, Cressida?' Miss Bronson asked again.

'For when I kiss boys, miss,' the girl whispered.

The headmistress arched an eyebrow. 'There is plenty of time to kiss boys when you are older, Cressida, when you have finished your examinations.'

'Yes, miss.'

I suppressed a smile.

'And Mr Merryman,' continued Miss Bronson, turning to me, 'who has quite enough to do around the school without adding the cleaning of the mirrors to his duties, has to wipe the mirror clean every time this silly girl kisses it.'

'It's a blasted nuisance, that's what it is,' growled the caretaker, brandishing his sponge before the girl.

'So, Mr Phinn,' continued Miss Bronson, 'I have invited Cressida to see what Mr Merryman has to do every time she kisses the mirror. If you will all accompany me.'

Miss Bronson led the way into the cloakroom. Facing us was a large mirror embellished with vivid red lip-shaped decorations.

'Perhaps you might demonstrate to Cressida what you have to do, Mr Merryman,' said the headmistress, 'every time she decides to kiss the mirror.'

The caretaker gripped the sponge, thrust it down a nearby lavatory bowl until it was wet, and then proceeded to wipe the mirror vigorously until is was clean.

'And he has to do that every time you kiss the mirror,' the headmistress told the girl in a rather sweet little voice. 'So you won't be doing it again, will you?'

It would be difficult to describe the look of utter revulsion on the face of poor Cressida.

☆ 20 ☆

ANGEL IN THE CLOAKROOM

Last week, when I was looking for my
PE kit in the cloakroom,
I saw an angel.
She was hovering above the coat
hooks, smiling at me
And waving a long white hand.
Her silver wings were trembling
And her golden halo shimmered in the sun.
This morning she was there again,
Smiling and shimmering,
Flapping and fluttering,
Waving and trembling.
She looked beautiful.

I told my teacher.
'Miss, there's an angel in the cloakroom.'
My teacher gave a little snort. 'An angel?'
She looked around the cloakroom but the
angel had gone.
'Too much television,' she sighed.
'Too lively an imagination.
A daydreamer, that's what you are.

Angels, indeed! Whatever next?'
She smiled and shook her head,
And then picked up a shining feather
  from the floor
And put it in the bin.

☆ **21** ☆

ROGER WRITES A POEM

The large red-brick primary school stood in the middle of a dreadfully depressing inner-city area. The work of the children consisted largely of arid exercises on the noun, the verb and the adjective but, when questioned, the children had not the first idea what the parts of speech were. Page after page was filled with dreary exercise after dreary exercise. There was the occasional story, the odd comprehension, but not a sign of a poem.

Roger sat in the corner, away from the other children, looking nervous and confused. I sat down next to him.

'May I look at your book?' I asked gently.

'Yes, sir,' he whispered, pushing a dog-eared exercise book in my direction. He watched me with a frightened, wide-eyed look. From the first page, I read an account entitled 'Myself'.

'Sir, we had to write that when we came to this school,' he explained quietly. 'Sir, so our teacher could get to know a bit about us. It's not very good. I'm not much good at writing.'

I'm not much good at anything realy. I like art but am not much good. I make lots of mistaks with my writting and I'm in the bottam set for everything. I've not realy got any friends. I dont realy like school. I cant do the work.

'It's not bad at all this, Roger,' I said, staring into his large, wide eyes. 'You just need to write a bit more and check your spellings and your punctuation.'

He nodded slowly.

Then, at the very back of the book, I came upon a piece of writing in small crabbed print. The content was very different from the rest of his work. I asked him if he had written it. He nodded. I asked him if he had received any help with it. He shook his head.

'This is very good,' I told him, much impressed.

The child looked surprised. 'Is it, sir?' he asked.

'It is,' I said, 'and I would like to make a copy. Sometimes, when I come across a very good piece of work in a school, I write it in my notebook.' I copied the spidery writing, reading it aloud as I did so:

Yesterday yesterday yesterday
Sorrow sorrow sorrow
Today today today
Hope hope hope
Tomorrow tomorrow tomorrow
Love love love

'What a wonderful little poem,' I told him.

He thought for a moment, stared up at me with those large, sad eyes and announced: 'They're mi spelling corrections, sir.'

☆ 22 ☆

MOLLY

AND THE MAGIC ROAD

I encountered Molly in the Infant classroom. She was a serious-faced girl with more paint on herself than on the large piece of paper in front of her. She had drawn what I thought was a snake: a long, multi-coloured creature that

curled and twisted across the page like a writhing serpent from a fairy story. It was a small masterpiece with intricate patterning and delightful detail.

'That's a very colourful snake,' I commented.

'It's not a snake,' the child told me, putting down her brush and folding her little arms across her chest. 'It's a road.'

'It looks like a snake to me.'

'Well, it's not. It's a road. I know cos I painted it.'

'Ah, yes, I can see now,' I said tactfully. 'Is it a magic road?'

'No.'

'It looks like a magic road to me.'

'Well, it isn't,' said the child. She placed her small hands on her hips. 'It's an ordinary road.'

'But it's full of greens and reds and blues. It looks like a magic road. Perhaps it leads beyond the ragged clouds to where the Snow Queen lives in her great white palace.'

The child observed me for a moment. 'It's an ordinary road and doesn't lead to any white palace.'

'Why all the colours?' I asked, intrigued.

Her finger traced the curve of the road. 'Those are the diamonds and those are the emeralds and those are the rubies,' she explained.

'It *is* a magic road!' I teased.

'No, it's not,' the child replied, 'it's a "jewel" carriageway.'

☆ 23 ☆

JOSEPH
AND THE SPECIAL PRESENT

The children were giving the teacher Easter presents at the end of term: chocolates and flowers, handkerchiefs and little bottles of perfume, small pottery figures and colourful scarves. One angelic-looking little girl presented the teacher with a small bag of sugar-coated chocolate eggs.

'These are for you, miss,' the child whispered sweetly, 'because you are my very favourite teacher.'

The teacher blushed with embarrassment and obvious pleasure. 'Oh, what a kind thought,' she said. 'Thank you so much, Amy.' She gave the child a peck on the cheek. 'Do you think I might have one now?'

The little girl nodded and watched as her teacher popped one of the chocolate eggs in her mouth.

A small boy then approached the teacher's desk with a little egg in the palm of his hand. 'This is for you, miss,' he said shyly.

'My goodness,' the teacher said, 'another present! Thank you so much, Joseph.' She then popped that egg in her mouth and crunched, just as the small boy announced proudly, 'Our budgie laid it this morning.'

☆ 24 ☆

PORTIA

THERE'S ALWAYS ONE

'This morning, we have a very special visitor with us,' said the teacher. She smiled and turned in my direction. 'Mr Phinn is a school inspector and he is very interested in what we are doing, aren't you, Mr Phinn?'

'I am,' I replied, smiling.

'He likes to sit in lessons and watch what children are doing, don't you, Mr Phinn?'

'I do,' I replied, keeping the smile fixed on my face.

'Now,' continued the teacher, 'because it is a Monday, we start the day as we normally do with "Newstime".' The teacher turned in my direction. 'It's an opportunity, Mr Phinn, for the children to tell us what they have been doing over the weekend. I don't know whether it's considered good practice or not these days. Things in education seem to shift like the sands of time.'

'It *is* good practice,' I reassured her, smiling still. 'It encourages the children to speak clearly, confidently and with enthusiasm.'

'Just what I think.' She nodded and proceeded. 'Well, this week, let me see whom I shall ask.' She scanned the classroom. 'Portia, would you like to come out to the front and tell us what interesting things you and your family have been doing over the weekend?'

A large, moon-faced, rather morose-looking girl with hair in enormous bunches and tied by large crimson ribbons, rose slowly from her seat and headed sluggishly for the front. She stared motionless at the class as if caught in amber, a grim expression on her round pale face.

'Come along, then, Portia,' urged the teacher.

'Nowt 'appened, miss,' the girl answered sullenly.

'Something must have happened, Portia. Did you go anywhere?'

'No, miss.'

''Well, what did you do all weekend?'

'Watch telly, miss.'

The teacher sighed and turned in my direction. 'It's like extracting teeth, getting some of the children to speak, Mr Phinn,' she confided in a *sotto voce* voice. 'Some of them are very economical in their use of words.' She turned her attention back to the large girl at the front of the classroom, who was staring vacantly out of the window. 'Now, come along, Portia, there must be something you can tell us?'

'Miss, we found an 'edge'og on our lawn on Saturday and it were dead,' the child announced bluntly.

'Oh dear,' said the teacher, pulling a dramatically sympathetic face. 'I wonder why that was. Do you think something could have killed it?' She then looked in my direction, an expectant expression playing about her eyes. 'Possibly a cat, Mr Phinn, do you think?'

'Very possibly,' I replied.

'My dad said it were probably next door's dog,' said Portia. 'It's allus killing things, that dog. My dad says it wants purrin down. It's a reight vicious thing. It bit 'im when 'e was fixing t'fence and last week it chased this old woman who were collecting for the RSPCA right down t'path. We could hear t'screaming from our back room.'

'Dear me, it does sound a rather fierce creature, Portia,' said the teacher.

'It bit 'er on t'bum by t'gate. All her little flags were ovver our garden and all down t'path. My dad said she wouldn't be coming back in an 'urry!'

'Well, well, how fascinating,' said the teacher, pulling a face and arching an eyebrow. 'Let's see if anyone else has any interesting news, shall we?'

Towards the end of the morning I took the opportunity, whilst the children were writing up their news, to look at the exercise books. Portia was writing carefully in large clear rounded letters as I approached her, but on catching sight of me she froze, dropped her pencil and stared up like a terrified rabbit in a trap.

'May I look at your work?' I asked gently. She slid the book across the desk, all the while staring. She had written the date at the top of the page in bold writing and then underneath in four large capital letters the word 'EGOG'.

'What does this say?' I asked.

'Can't you read?' she said bluntly.

'I'm not so sure about that word,' I told her, pointing to the title.

''Edge'og!' she replied, looking at me as if I was incredibly stupid.

Try as I might, I just couldn't get her to speak to me above the single word so I tried another tack, to reassure her that I was really quite friendly.

'It's a lovely name, Portia,' I said. She eyed me suspiciously. 'You were named after one of the most famous characters in a wonderful play by William Shakespeare. Portia was a very clever and beautiful woman.'

I was about to launch into a rendering of 'The quality of mercy is not strained' when the teacher approached, bent low so her lips were nearly in my ear and informed me in slow and deliberate tones that 'The name is spelled "P-O-R-S-C-H-E" not "P-O-R-T-I-A", Mr Phinn. Her father told me, when I asked him about the unusual spelling one Parents' Evening, that he always wanted a Porsche car but couldn't afford one. She's the next best thing.' Mrs Peterson shook her head, shrugged and mouthed: 'There's always one!'

☆ 25 ☆

DREAMING

In the corner of the classroom,
A small child stared at the stuffed hedgehog
In the glass case.

'What are you thinking about?' asked the school
inspector.
'I was just wondering,' the child replied wistfully,
'What it was doing . . . before it was stuffed!'

☆ 26 ☆

BENEDICT
A PRECOCIOUS CHILD

As I entered the Infant classroom I was approached by a small serious-faced boy with bright blue eyes magnified behind large, framed glasses. His curly blond hair stuck out at the sides like earmuffs.

'You must be the school inspector?' he said with all the precocious confidence of a six-year-old.

'Yes, that's right,' I replied.

'Mr Phinn.'

'Yes, indeed.'

'We've been expecting you. Have you travelled far?'

'Not too far,' I told him, marvelling at his self-assurance. It is rare that one so young approaches the strange visitor in the black suit and with a clipboard. The children, as indeed the teachers, are usually in awe of the school inspector.

'I've been looking forward to meeting you,' the small boy told me.

'Really?'

'Yes, we've been reading some of your poems in class and I have to say that I find them quite delightful.'

I have come across many a bright little button on my travels around schools but this one sparkled.

'That's very kind of you. Every writer likes to hear such praise. I am pleased you enjoyed them. And what is your name?'

'I'm Benedict,' he told me, holding out a small hand which I shook formally.

'Well, Benedict, shouldn't you be getting on with your work?'

'I've done it. When we've finished our writing, we're allowed to select a book from the Reading Corner. I was on my way there when I thought I'd stop and say hello.'

His manner and speech were amusingly old-fashioned for one so young.

'Well, that's very nice of you, Benedict,' I said.

The small boy studied me carefully for a moment with those penetrating blue eyes. 'Mrs McGuire – she's our teacher, but you probably know that already – well, Mrs McGuire says there are much better words to use than "nice".'

'I'm sure she's right,' I said, chuckling. 'I'll try to remember in future.'

'And that there are much more interesting words to use in our stories than "said". Do you like stories, Mr Phinn?'

'I do,' I replied.

'Would you like to see some of mine?'

'Perhaps later, Benedict,' I told him. 'I'm a little busy at the moment.'

'Righto, I'll get along then and choose a book. I like poetry, you know. I love the rhymes.' He thought for a moment and then said, 'Do you know, Mr Phinn, we've had a very interesting conversation, haven't we?'

'We have, Benedict,' I replied, 'indeed we have.'

He then patted me gently on the arm and said, before departing for the Reading Corner, 'We must do lunch sometime.'

☆ 27 ☆

MARY
IN TEARS

When I arrived at school that cold December morning to watch the rehearsal for the Nativity play, I came across a small girl of about seven or eight, surrounded by a group of much bigger girls. The child was wailing in the most pitiful way and rubbing her little eyes to stem the tears. My first thought was that she was being bullied.

'Whatever's the matter?' I asked.

'We're not supposed to talk to strangers,' a large frizzy-haired girl told me sharply. 'If you don't clear off, we'll tell Mrs Holbrook.'

'Stranger danger!' shouted another child.

'I'm the school inspector,' I told the group quickly. 'I'm here to see Mrs Holbrook and to see the Nativity play.'

At the mention of the Nativity play the distressed child gave a great howl.

'Have you any means of identification?' the frizzy-haired girl demanded.

I produced my official details which she scrutinized.

'My gran says you can't be too careful,' she told me before thrusting them back to me.

'Why is this little girl crying?' I asked.

'Cos she's dead upset.'

'I can see that,' I told her, 'but why?'

'Because her name's Mary,' I was told by another child.

'And why should that make her cry?' I asked. 'Mary is a lovely name.'

'She was all right until we started doing the flipping Nativity play,' explained the frizzy-haired girl. 'Then the lads started to call her names.'

The centre of all the attention suddenly stopped crying. She snivelled and whimpered and took a deep breath. Then she told me, 'They keep calling me virgin, and I'm not.'

☆ 28 ☆

CHARLIE
THE REMEDIAL CHILD

Charlie, a small boy of about ten or eleven, was sitting at his desk by the window poring over his book, his brow furrowed in concentration. As I approached, he closed the book and placed a hand firmly on top.

'May I look at your work?' I asked, smiling.

'No,' came the blunt reply.

'Why not?' I asked.

'Because tha not lookin', that's why. It's no good. When t'teacher says, "Today, we're doin' writing", I don't feel all that well. Me stomach gets all churned up like. I have problems with me writing, you see. Me spelling's not up to much and me handwriting's all ovver t'place.'

'I'd still like to see,' I said.

'Well, tha not.' He kept a firm hand over his book so I could not verify his comments. 'Can't read reight well, either,' he added. 'I have trouble wi' words.'

'I see,' I replied gently.

He looked me full in the face. 'I'm remedial, tha knows.'

'And what does that mean?' I asked, knowing full well the meaning of the label sometimes attached to children with special educational needs.

'Thick,' he replied bluntly. Then he added sadly, 'I'm not much good at owt really.'

'Everyone's good at something,' I said.

He just shook his head in a resigned sort of way and stared out of the window to the distant hills.

'Tha not from round 'ere then?' he asked.

'No, I live at the other side of the dale.'

'Aye, I thowt by way yer were speakin' you were an off-comed-un.'

Since starting work in rural Yorkshire, I had been called this more times than I can remember – someone from out of the dale, a foreigner. 'I am indeed an "off-comed-un",' I admitted.

I hoped, by changing the subject, I might eventually prevail upon the boy to show me his work and answer a few questions so I asked, 'Where do you live?'

'Reight up theer.' He pointed through the window to the far-off hills. 'I live on a farm up theer – at t'top of t'dale.'

'What a lucky boy you are,' I murmured. 'You must have one of the finest views in the world.'

'It's all reight,' he said in a matter-of-fact voice. 'What time were you up this mornin' then, mester?'

'Early,' I replied. 'Half past six.'

'I was up at six helpin' me dad deliver a calf.'

'Really?'

'And it were dead. It would've been a good milker an' all, just like its mother, wide solid rear and good udder texture. We got ratchet on –'

'Ratchet?' I interrupted.

'Aye, you put yer ratchet up against t'cow, it's a sort of metal gadget like. Yer tie yer ropes round yer calf's back legs and yer turn yer ratchet every time there's a contraction. Helping cow along a bit.' He paused. 'Does tha know what a contraction is?'

'I do,' I replied.

'Aye, it were dead all reight. So we've 'ad a month of it, I can tell thee,' continued Charlie, fixing his eyes on a flock of sheep meandering between the grey limestone walls. He sighed and was quiet for a moment. 'Them's ours,' he then remarked casually, 'them sheep. We've got an 'undred yows and two jocks.'

'Jocks?' I asked. 'Are they Scottish sheep?'

He shook his head and dusty mop of hair. 'No, no, jocks are rams, moor sheep. Does tha know why we 'as all them yows and only the two jocks?'

'Yes,' I replied, smiling, 'I think so.'

'Bought another from t'market last week. It'd only been wi' us three days and it dropped down dead – even before it had done any tuppin',' he continued. 'Me dad were none too pleased.' He paused fractionally and gave a low whistle between his teeth. 'Does tha know what tuppin' means?'

'Yes,' I replied.

'We'd trouble week afore wi' 'oggits.'

'Hoggits? Little pigs?' I ventured.

He shook his head again. 'No, no, your 'oggits are sheep of an age between your lamb and your ewe. Sort of teen-age sheep.' He observed me for a moment. 'Does tha know what a drape is?'

'No, I don't,' I replied.

'A stirk?'

'I'm afraid not,' I told him.

'Tha dunt know much, does tha?' he said, shaking his head.

'No,' I agreed. 'I'm remedial, you know.'

He looked at me thoughtfully and a smile formed on his lips for the first time that morning. 'I don't know owt abaat that but tha're an off-comed-un and no mistake.'

'I am,' I admitted. Then, like a sensitive and patient teacher, the child who was 'nowt much good at owt', who 'had trouble wi' words', invited the off-comed-un, the school inspector who had his own 'special educational needs', into his world of hoggits and shearlings, stots and stirks, wethers and tups, tegs and hogs, becoming animated as he realized the extent of his companion's ignorance, surprised that there were people who couldn't tell a Blue-faced Leicester from a Texel or a Masham from a Swaledale.

'We've a sheepdog what's going blind and t'last straw were this calf. It would've been a reight good milker an' all.'

'I'm sorry to hear about all your troubles.' My reply sounded feeble.

'Me dad's got a word for it.' At that point I felt it wise to move on but he reassured me. 'Oh, it's not rude. It's a word which describes a yow when she's heavy pregnant, so heavy, you see, she falls over on her back and just can't move, she's helpless. Sticks her legs in t'air and just can't shift. It's called "rigged", proper word is "riggwelted". Me dad comes in from t'fields and flops on t'settee and says, "I'm fair riggwelted."'

Some weeks later I was asked to speak at a very prestigious educational conference in London. Following my lecture, I was approached by the Minister of Education who enquired, 'And how are things in education in the North of England, Mr Phinn?'

'Well,' I replied, smiling mischievously, 'the teachers are feeling somewhat "riggwelted".'

☆ 29 ☆

IMOGEN
HAS TROUBLE WITH HER Rs

In the nursery, I met Imogen. She looked like a china doll: golden curls, huge blue eyes and a flawless complexion. The child was casually turning the pages of an early reader. Each page displayed an object: house, bus, church, man, woman, dog, car and so on, beneath which was the word in large black letters.

'Will you read it to me, please?' she asked.

'Of course,' I replied, amused by such a confident little thing.

'I know some words,' she told me, 'but I can't read all of them.'

When I had finished reading the book, I wrote the word 'car' on a piece of paper. 'Now,' I said, 'can you read this word for me?'

'No, I can't,' she replied.

'It begins with a curly "c". We've just read it in the book. Would you like to have a guess?'

'No, I can't read it.'

'Let me give you a clue,' I said. 'Your daddy or mummy might drive you to school in it in the morning.'

'Oh yes!' she cried. 'You mean Wolls-Woyce.'

☆ 30 ☆

SPELLING

The inspector asked the little ones,
'Can anyone tell me
A word that begins with the letter Q?'
And a child said, 'Quistmas twee.'

☆ QUESTION ☆

'What is the point,' asked Dad,
'Of having a stud through your tongue?'

'If you mutht know,' replied his daughter, 'I'm exthprething my perthonality.'

☆ 31 ☆

SHANE & WAYNE
PREPARE FOR MOTHER'S DAY

In the Junior classroom, tucked away in a corner, were two boys busy sewing. One looked as if he had been dragged through a hedge backwards. He had spiky hair, a round red face and large ears. His nose was running and a front tooth was missing. His shirt was hanging out, his socks were concertinaed around his ankles, his legs were covered in cuts and bruises, and his shoes were so scuffed I couldn't tell whether they were originally black or brown. His hands and face were both entirely innocent of soap and water. His companion looked as healthy as a prize-winning bull. He was a very large, amiable-looking boy with a round moon of a face, great dimpled elbows and knees, and fingers as fat as sausages. Both boys were surrounded by threads, cottons, fabrics, an assortment of needles, boxes of pins and scissors and both were sewing furiously, their arms rising and falling like pistons.

'Hello,' I said brightly.

'Hello,' replied the larger boy. His companion continued to sew with a vengeance, his eyes narrowed in concentration.

'And how are you?'

'Middlin' well,' replied the large boy. 'I'm Shane and he's Wayne.'

'And what are you two up to?' I asked.

'Samplers!' said the boy, not taking his eyes off the sewing for a second.

'Samplers?'

'Victorian embroidery,' the toothless one informed me, still vigorously sewing, 'for flipping Mother's Day on Sunday.' He did not look all that happy.

'I see,' I said, bending over them to get a closer look at their work. 'May I see?'

'Can't be stopping,' said the toothless one, continuing to sew with great determination, forcing the needle savagely through the canvas. 'Got to get it finished.' He turned to his friend. 'Pass us t'pink will tha, Shane?'

His companion searched through the assortment of coloured threads. 'All gone,' he replied bluntly.

'All gone!' exclaimed the toothless boy. 'All gone! Tha's gone and used up all t'pink?'

'I needed it for mi roses.'

'And tha's used all t'purple, an all?'

'That were for mi lilac.'

'And t'yella?'

'That were for mi daffs,' said the large boy apologetically.

'And tha's left me wi' all t'blacks and t'browns and t'greys. Thanks very much, Shane!'

The boys, entirely oblivious of my presence, resumed pushing the large needles through the fabric as if their lives depended upon it.

'Just stop a moment, will you, please,' I told them.

The toothless one paused, looked up, wiped the dewdrop from his nose with the back of his hand and then returned to his sewing as if he had not heard me.

'I can't stop,' he told me. 'I've got to gerrit done.'

His companion, clearly very pleased with his effort, held up a pale square of cream fabric. In large, uneven letters were the words: A MOTHER'S LOVE IS A BLESSING. The border was ablaze with a whole host of large, unrecognizable but extremely vivid flowers.

'I've just got mi name to put at t'bottom and I'm all done,' he announced proudly.

'And tha's used up all t'pink,' grumbled his companion, who was still stitching away madly, 'and purples and yellas.'

The large boy straightened his sampler with a fat, pink hand and admired his handiwork before asking, 'Are you one of these school inspectors our teacher was on about?'

'I am,' I replied.

'What do you reckon to mi sampler, then?'

'Well, it's very bright and original but, you know, if I had come into your school a hundred years ago, you'd have been in real trouble.'

'How old are you, then?' asked the toothless boy.

'What I meant is that if a school inspector had visited your school at the time it was built, you would have been in trouble.'

'Why's that then?'

'Because your stitches are too big. If you look at the

Victorian samplers, you will notice that the lettering and designs are very delicate and very carefully stitched.'

The toothless boy stopped sewing abruptly, examined his sampler and carefully put down his needle and thread, before turning to look me straight in the face. 'Aye, well, if I did 'em all small and delicate like what you say, mi mum'd nivver gerrit, would she? I've been on this for four week and I'll be lucky to get it done for next year's Mother's Day, way things stand.'

'I'll get mine done,' Shane chimed in smugly.

'Aye!' snapped the toothless one. 'And we know why, don't we?'

'Why?' I asked.

'Because, when Miss give out all these different Victorian sayings and proverbs, I was off poorly and when I got back I was stuck wi' t'one nob'dy wanted. Shane got t'shortest – A MOTHER'S LOVE IS A BLESSING – and I got t'longest!' He displayed his piece of fabric with a grubby finger. It read:

THERE IS NOTHING SO PURE,
THERE IS NOTHING SO HIGH,
AS THE LOVE YOU WILL SEE
IN YOUR MOTHER'S EYE.

'I've only just started mi border,' he moaned. 'And Shane's used all t'pinks and t'yellas and t'purples and I'm stuck wi' t'blacks, t'browns and t'greys!'

'You could do animals instead of flowers,' suggested his companion with a self-satisfied smirk on his moon-shaped face. 'You don't need colours for sheep and cows and goats . . .'

'I'd need summat for t'pigs, though, wouldn't I?' cried the toothless one. 'And tha's used all t'pink!'

'I'm sure that, however it turns out, your mother will love your sampler,' I reassured him.

'If she gets it!' he barked.

'Well, I may see you boys later,' I said, moving away.

'Later?' they exclaimed in unison.

'I thought I'd pop into the Singing class during the lunch-hour,' I told them.

'Singing!' the toothless one exclaimed. 'Singing! We don't gu to no Singing class! That's for t'cissies!'

The other boy, putting the finishing touches to his large pink rose, nodded in agreement before echoing his companion's sentiments: 'Aye, choir's for t'cissies and t'lasses. You wunt catch us theer.'

As I headed to another desk, I heard a plaintive cry from the corner table, 'Miss, miss, can I have some pink thread, please? We're clean out over 'ere!'

☆ 32 ☆

HYACINTH

THE CHILD WITH SPECIAL NEEDS

I found Hyacinth poring over a large picture book at her desk.

'Hello,' I said.

The girl wiped her nose with the back of a finger and eyed me apprehensively.

'Let's see what you are doing, shall we?' She didn't object as I slid her reading book across the desk and started to examine it.

'Is it a good book?' I asked.

She looked at me suspiciously but didn't answer.

'Would you like to read a little of your book to me?' I asked.

She shook her head, gazing at me now with unabashed intensity. She wiped her nose on her finger again and then told me in a loud voice, 'I'm special needs.' Perhaps she thought that this revelation might convince me to leave her in peace. When I didn't move, she added, 'Don't you know? I'm special needs.'

'I do, but what do you think it means, special needs?'

'If you know what it means, why are you askin'?'

It was a fair question. 'So, will you read to me?'

'Are you the infector?' she asked.

'Inspector,' I replied.

'Can't see t'difference,' she mumbled.

Hyacinth reluctantly read to me, slowly and with fierce concentration on her face, her finger following each word on the page. There was no expression in her voice and not once did she pause for breath but read on, determined to get the ordeal over and done with.

'Hyacinth,' I said, when she closed the book with a bang, 'that was very good, but what do you do when you come to a full stop?'

'What?'

'When you get to a full stop, what do you do?'

She eyed me like an expert in the presence of an ignoramus. 'You gerroff t'bus,' she replied.

☆ 33 ☆

THOMAS

A BOY OF FEW WORDS

Thomas was a child of the dales. He was a small boy with a crown of close-cropped fair hair and large pale eyes between almost colourless lashes. I have met many a good little reader on my visits to schools and he was one of the best. He read from his book with grim determination in a loud and confident voice.

'You're a very good reader,' I commented when he snapped the book shut.

'Aye,' he replied, nodding sagely.

'Do you like reading?'

'I do.'

'And I see from your reading card you've read a lot of books this year.'

'I have.'

'Do you read at home?'

'Sometimes.'

It was like extracting blood from a stone but I persevered. 'And what do you like reading about?' I asked cheerfully.

'Animals mostly.'

'Farm animals? Wild animals?'

'All animals.'

'And do you have any animals at home?'

'A few.'

'What sort?' I asked.

'Mostly black and white on green.'

'Pardon?'

'Cows,' he said quietly. 'I live on a farm.' Then a slight smile came to his lips and his expression took on a sort of patient, sympathetic, tolerant look.

'Do you know owt about cows, then?' he asked.

'No,' I said feebly. I should have left it there but I persisted. 'Would you like to tell me about the cows on your farm?'

'There's not that much to tell really, cows is cows.'

'You're not a very talkative little boy, are you?' I said, peering into the pale eyes.

'If I've got owt to say I says it, and if I've got owt to ask I asks it,' he replied casually.

☆ 34 ☆

DARREN
CHALLENGES THE VICAR

The vicar started his assembly by asking the children to try and guess what was in his head. He told them that as he had walked through the churchyard on his way to the school that morning, he had seen something in a tree.

'You know, children,' he said, 'I had such a surprise. There it was, poking its little grey head between the branches of the great oak tree, its great bushy tail twitching and its little darting, black, shiny eyes like beads staring at me.' He paused for effect. Then his gaze settled on Darren, a large boy with very fair hair, who was sitting at the front of the hall. 'Now, young man,' said the cleric smiling, 'what do you think I'm talking about?'

'Well, I know it's Jesus,' replied the boy, 'but it sounds very like a squirrel to me.'

☆ 35 ☆

BIBLE CLASS

Reverend Bright, our vicar,
Came to our class today.
He started with a little talk,
Then we closed our eyes to pray.
He talked about the Bible,
And the prophet Abraham,
How God created everything
And how the world began.
Then he asked us all some questions
About the prophets and the kings,
David and Goliath,
And lots of other things.
'In a very famous garden
Grew an apple on a tree,
And who ate the forbidden fruit?'
And a voice said:

'Wasn't me!'

☆ 36 ☆

PAIGE AND THE NUMERACY WORKSHEET

I approached a small girl busily writing away with a large pencil.

'And what's your name?' I asked.

'Paige,' she replied, continuing to write.

'That's a nice name,' I said.

'My granny doesn't like it.'

'Well, I do,' I said. 'It's unusual, like mine.' Glancing at the top of the child's work, where she had printed her name, I could see why her grandmother was not too keen. The girl was called Paige Turner. Poor child, I thought. 'May I ask you what you're doing, Paige?' I asked.

'I'm doing a numeracy worksheet,' she told me. The girl glanced behind her to see where the teacher was before adding, 'It's really sums but we have to call it numeracy now.'

'I see.'

'And we have to call English literacy.'

'Really?'

'I've done this worksheet twice before. All my answers are right.'

'Why have you done this worksheet twice before?' I asked, intrigued.

'Because we've got to get it all right. We've got school inspectors in this week, didn't you know?'

I smiled. She was clearly unaware of who I was. 'I see,' I said.

'We've been practising all our work for the last two weeks so that we get everything right. Miss says that if we get one of these school inspectors in the room we've got to be on our best behaviour or they could send us to another school. Oh, and if we know the answer to a question we put our right hand up and if we don't know the answer then we put our left hand up, then she'll know who to ask. And she said if we're really really good then we'll all get some chocolate at the end of the week.'

'Do you know to whom you are speaking?' I asked the child.

'Course I do. You're Debbie's granddad, come in to help with the slow readers.'

I examined the worksheet. The children had been set the exercise of identifying different geometrical shapes –

squares, rectangles, circles, triangles and so on – which had been drawn on a piece of paper.

Paige had completed the first two questions correctly: 'Is this a triangle or a circle?' and 'Is this a square or a rectangle?' but in answer to the third question she had written what looked like 'Melanie'.

'What is this word?' I queried.

'Melanie,' replied the child.

'Melanie,' I repeated, puzzled. 'Why have you written "Melanie"?'

'Well, it says, "Name this shape",' she replied sweetly, 'so I thought I'd call it Melanie.'

☆ 37 ☆

STEVIE

IN TROUBLE AGAIN

Mrs Gardiner, the headteacher, was a stout woman in her late fifties with a large bust and remarkably narrow waist. She wore a long blue skirt, a pale pink blouse and around her neck hung a pair of gold half-moon spectacles on a thin gold chain.

She stood before the little boy in queenly fashion, straight-backed and dramatically tight-lipped, her hands clasped in front of her.

'Not you again, Stevie,' she sighed, shaking her head.

'Yes, miss,' replied the boy sheepishly. He looked up at her with large round eyes.

He was a cheeky-looking little lad with a face full of freckles, a runny nose and short ginger hair. His tie was skew-whiff, his grubb white shirt was hanging out of his trousers and his jumper had large holes at the elbows.

'Don't look at me as if butter wouldn't melt in your mouth, young man,' the headteacher told him sternly.

The boy looked down at his old, scuffed shoes.

'Whatever are we going to do with you?' asked the headteacher. She did not really expect an answer for she continued without a pause. 'Every week, every week,' she repeated, 'you are sent to my room for one thing or another.'

'Yes, miss,' murmured the boy, looking up with a sad expression on his face.

'You are always in trouble. You attract misfortune like a human magnet. Last week, it was running down the corridor and nearly knocking the caretaker off his ladder.'

'Yes, miss,' said the boy quietly.

'The week before you let the dog into school, and it wasn't that long ago that you let the hamster out of the cage and we spent the whole day trying to get it from under the floorboards.'

'Yes, miss.'

'Then there was the incident with the fire extinguisher only a day after you managed to pull all the tins off the top shelf in Mrs Farringdon's storeroom, covering the teacher in powder paint.'

The boy remained silent but shuffled his feet nervously.

'You're a real nuisance, Stevie Simcox,' snapped Mrs Gardiner. 'A pest, an irritation, a very, very naughty boy.'

'Yes, miss.'

'And you know that I am leaving next week, at the end of the term, to go to another school?'

'Yes, miss.'

'Well, I will tell you this, Stevie, I shall miss a great deal about Crompton Primary School but there is one person I shall not miss at all and that is you. I feel sorry for the new headteacher having such a troublesome little boy to deal with every week.'

'Yes, miss.'

'And what is it now?' demanded the headteacher. 'Why are you outside my door yet again?'

The boy held up an envelope.

'What's this?' asked the headteacher, snatching it from his hands.

'It's a leaving card, miss,' the child told her. 'I got it you to wish you good luck in your new school.'

☆ 38 ☆

SIMONE & WILLIAM
LEARN TO SPEAK PROPER

I was spending the morning in a primary school set high up in the dales, and was looking at the work of the six- and seven-year-olds. As I looked through one little boy's book, a red-cheeked lass nearby piped up, 'Miss, I can't find mi readin' book. I don't know weer I've gone an' putten it.'

'I cannot find my reading book,' the teacher repeated slowly and precisely, 'because I do not know where I have put it.'

'That's wor I just said, miss. I've gorran putten it down someweer an' I don't know weer I've putten it.'

'I have put it down somewhere, Simone,' corrected the teacher, 'but I do not know where I have put it.'

'Have ya, miss?' the child asked innocently. 'Did *you* 'ave mi book, then?'

'No, *you* have put it down,' the teacher said, drawing a deep exasperated breath.

'I know, miss, that's wor I just said,' the girl answered, screwing up her nose.

'There is no such word, Simone, as "putten",' the teacher explained. 'The word is "put". "I have put down my book" and not "I have putten down my book."'

'Miss!' another child piped up. 'She's gone an' putten it on *my* desk. It's 'ere.'

'Put, William, put,' the teacher corrected sharply. The teacher sighed dramatically. 'You know, Mr Phinn,' she said, 'sometimes I really ask myself why I bother.' I asked myself the self-same question. 'I think I am fighting a losing battle,' she continued, 'trying to get the children to speak properly.' I was certain she was right in that as well.

Just before morning break, the teacher wrote a sentence in large white letters on the blackboard: 'I have putten my book on the teacher's desk.'

'Now, children,' she said, facing the class. 'Look this way, please. On the blackboard I have written a sentence. Who can tell me what is wrong with it?'

Young William waved his hand backwards and forwards in the air like a lupin in a strong wind. 'I know, miss!' he shouted out.

'Yes, William, what is wrong with the sentence, "I have putten my book on the teacher's desk"?'

'Miss,' the boy replied, 'tha's gone and putten "putten" when tha should 'ave putten "put".'

☆ 39 ☆

MATTHEW
AND THE DINOSAURS

By the window a grubby but bright-eyed little boy was splashing paint onto a large piece of sugar paper.

'Hullo, what are you doing?' I asked.

'Paintin'!' came the blunt reply.

'It looks very good.'

'We dunt paint much,' the child said. 'Only we are today. We've got an important visitor coming.' There had been no thought in the boy's mind that the important visitor might be me.

'And what are you painting?' I asked.

'It's a jungle,' came the reply. 'Prehistoric.'

'What's that creature?'

'Brontosaurus.'

'And that?'

'Triceratops. They 'ad three 'orns on their 'eads, tha knows. Did tha' know that?'

'Yes.'

'This one's a pterodactyl and over 'ere's a pteranadon. A lot of people don't know t'difference, tha knows. Do you?'

'Yes.'

'Well, a lot of people don't.'

'What's this one?' I asked, pointing to a round, fat, smiling creature.

'Stegosaurus. They had three brains, tha knows.'

'Really?'

'One in their 'ead, one in their tail and one in their bum. It din't do 'em any good though.' The boy had pointed to a vicious-looking monster with spikes along its back and great sharp teeth like vicious tank traps. 'He ate 'em all – Tyrannosaurus rex. He were reight nasty, he was.'

'You know a lot about these creatures,' I said.

'I know.' The little boy put down his brush. 'I luv 'em. They're great. I draw 'em all t'time.'

'And are there any around today?'

'Course not! They're all dead. They're hextinct.'
'What does that mean?'
'Dead. Wiped aaht.'
'And why do you think that is?' I asked.
The little boy had thought for a moment. 'Well, mister,' he said, 'that's one of life's gret mysteries, in't it?'

☆ 40 ☆

USING YOUR IMAGINATION

On Monday, Miss Cawthorne
Said we could paint a picture
And all use our imaginations.
I drew a dragon
In a dark and dripping cave,
With yellow scaly skin
And slithery, snake-like tail,
Blue fins and bone-white horns,
Red-eyed and breathing purple flames.
But Miss Cawthorne, when she saw it, sighed and said,
'Dominic, dear, dragons are not yellow.
They are green!'

read more

GERVASE PHINN

A WAYNE IN A MANGER

Gervase Phinn recollects his favourite Christmas and Nativity stories from the time he was a schools inspector for English and Drama in the Yorkshire Dales. Joyous and hilarious, *A Wayne in a Manger* reminds us that even the most famous story doesn't always end the way we expect.

A Wayne in a Manger includes some wonderfully funny and touching anecdotes about Nativity plays, including disastrous ad-libbing, and children forgetting their lines, falling off the stage and showing their knickers. One story tells of an Innkeeper who generously says there's plenty of room for Mary and Joseph in the inn, while another Innkeeper, jealous of Joseph's starring role, allows Mary to come in but tells Joseph he can 'push off'. There's the story about the doll used as the Baby Jesus who suddenly pipes up with 'My name is Tammy. Are you my mommy?' And there's Mary who tells Joseph, 'I'm having a baby – oh, and it's not yours.'

'Hilarious and hair-raising' *Sunday Times*

'For anyone who has ever attended an infant nativity play and cried silent tears – of laughter' *Daily Express*

'Heart-warming ... will delight anyone who's sat at the back of the school hall to watch infants in their first stage role' *Family Circle*

'An enchanting collection of anecdotes' *Woman's Own*

GERVASE PHINN

THE OTHER SIDE OF THE DALE

Gervase Phinn is offered the position of schools inspector for English and Drama in the Yorkshire Dales because of his good sense and lack of pretension. As he reveals in this warm and humorous account, the first year in his job was quite an educational experience.

He quickly learns that he must slow his pace, and spend time appreciating the glorious Dales countryside – 'Backwatersthwaite's been theer since time o' Vikings. It'll still be theer when thee finds it.' He meets some larger-than-life characters, from farmers to lords of the manor, from teaching nuns to eccentric caretakers. And best of all, he discovers the endearing and disarming qualities of the Dales children.

OVER HILL AND DALE

'Miss, who's that funny man at the back of the classroom?' So begins schools inspector Gervase Phinn's second year among the frankly spoken pupils of North Yorkshire. He finds himself confronting Mr Swan, whose hunger for his lunch exceeds his appetite for English; unwittingly plays the stooge to Mrs Peterson's junior class; and is alarmingly disarmed by a pupil unsure whether he is learning French or German.

But Gervase is far from daunted. He is still in pursuit of Christine Bentley, the lovely headteacher of Winnery Nook School; he's ready to brave the steely glare of the officious Mrs Savage, and even feels up to helping Dr Gore organize a gathering of Feoffees – just as soon as someone tells him who or what they are.

This is a delectable second helping of hilarious tales from the man who has been dubbed 'the James Herriot of schools'. It will have you laughing out loud.

GERVASE PHINN

HEAD OVER HEELS IN THE DALES

Gervase Phinn thought he'd heard just about everything in his two years as a schools inspector, but a surprising enquiry from an angelic six-year-old reminds him never to take children for granted: 'Could you tell me how to spell sex, please?'

This year, however, he has other more important things on his mind beside schools. His impending marriage to Christine Bentley, the prettiest headteacher for miles around, finding themselves somewhere to live in the idyllic Yorkshire Dales, and the chance of promotion, all generate their fair share of excitement. But it's in the classroom that Gervase faces his greatest challenge – keeping a straight face as teachers and children alike conspire to have him, and us, laughing out loud.

UP AND DOWN IN THE DALES

Now in his fourth year as an inspector for English and Drama in the Yorkshire Dales, Gervase Phinn still relishes visiting the schools – whether an inner-city comprehensive fraught with difficulties or a small village primary school where the main danger is one of closure. With endless good humour, he copes with the little surprises that occur round every corner.

Some things never change, however: Mrs Savage roars, Connie rants, and Gervase's colleagues in the Inspectors' Office play verbal ping-pong. But all this can be put behind him when he returns home each evening to his lovely wife Christine, who is expecting their first baby. One day, their child will surely take the limelight in the local primary school where the children's contrived innocence never fails to win over even the hardest heart.

GERVASE PHINN

THE HEART OF THE DALES

Awkward teachers, pompous school governors and fearsome lollipop ladies might make Gervase Phinn's job as a Yorkshire schools inspector difficult but, as always, the guileless children prove his real challenge.

The new school year doesn't get off to the best start, however, when a teacher suggests Gervase has let him and his school down. Called up in front of his new boss, the formidable Miss de la Mare, Gervase fears he's in hot water. To add to his woes, he is given a 'little job' by Dr Gore, which means liaising with the infuriating Mrs Savage, the bane of the inspectors' lives.

Meanwhile, away from schools and the office, Gervase's family life is blissful – and not even strange night-time noises in the attic can upset the harmony of such a happy family.

What the critics have said about GERVASE PHINN:

'The James Herriot of schools ... Gervase Phinn writes warmly and with great wit' *Sunday Express*

'A born racconteur' *Guardian*

'Gervase Phinn is a natural story-teller ... He has a marvellous ear for one-liners and a constant flow of anecdotes about things children say' *Yorkshire Post*

'Uproarious and touching by turns, Gervase Phinn writes with enormous warmth and wit about his romantic adventures, career struggles and the children in the schools he visits' *Daily Mail*

'Phinn writes with that smooth, deceptively easy fluency which is the hallmark of quality. Combine this with a seemingly inexhaustible fund of anecdotes, peopled by characters brought to life with warmth, humour and affection, and the result is as delightful as it is inevitable' *Yorkshire Evening Post*
